Stronger
than
Anxiety

Also by Alexandra Vasiliu

Poetry Books
Dare to Let Go
Healing Is a Gift
Time to Heal
Healing Words
Be My Moon
Magnetic
Blooming
Through the Heart's Eyes

Children's Books
My Love Will Stay Forever
You Can Do Amazing Things
Dear Snowman
Have You Seen a Kangaroo Saying:
'How Do You Do?'

Journals
Plant Hope

Stronger
than
Anxiety

Poems about Overcoming Negative Thoughts,
Defeating Self-Sabotage,
and Building Self-Confidence

Alexandra Vasiliu

Stairway Books
2024

For those who want to overcome their fears.

***

Stronger than Anxiety: Poems about Overcoming Negative Thoughts, Defeating Self-Sabotage, and Building Self-Confidence by Alexandra Vasiliu. Stairway Books, 2024
ISBN-13: 978-1-963003-00-0 (paperback)
ISBN-13: 978-1-963003-01-7 (ebook)
ISBN-13: 978-1-963003-02-4 (hardcover)
First paperback edition, November 2024
Editing services provided by Melanie Underwood at
www.melanieunderwood.co.uk
Cover Illustration: Bebee via Canva Professional www.canva.com
Illustrations used under license from Shutterstock www.shutterstock.com

Alexandra Vasiliu

Author's Preface

This book is a work of love and generosity written only for you. It is my gift to you. Pieces of my heart are poured into each word, poem, and page. That is my humble way of telling you: *Don't cry. I am with you. You are fully seen and heard. You are not alone. I stand by you.*

Anxiety, negative thinking, self-doubt, and self-sabotage are universal experiences, yet love, empathy, understanding, and acceptance are the unique denominators for strong characters and good friends.

I hope these poems create an emotional bond and connect us despite life's harsh circumstances. *I am with you. You are fully seen and heard. You are not alone. I stand by you.*

Alexandra Vasiliu

May my poems be your steadfast companion on your journey, illuminating your path and mind and offering you strength, confidence, and encouragement every step of the way. You are a beautiful soul who deserves all these amazing things and so much more.
I stand by you.

With love,
Alexandra

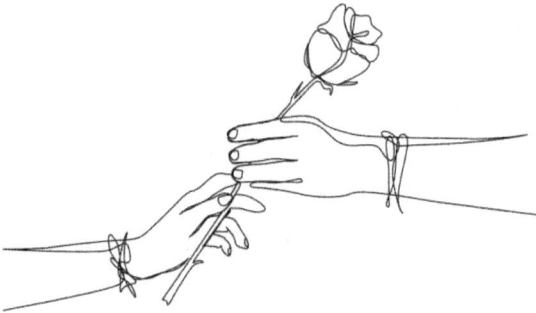

Take My Words with You

If you are struggling with anxiety,
I hope
you can rest
in the heart of my poems.
Deep down there,
I hid pieces of wisdom
for you –
small gems.

Alexandra Vasiliu

When you discover them,
hold onto them.
Absorb my uplifting words
with grace and bravery.
They will also keep you safe
and nurture your heart with strength,
courage,
peace,
and love.
I humbly offer you my poems
as friendly and healing hugs.
Let them embrace you compassionately.
I am sure
one day,
you will be able to release anxiety
as you would forget
and leave behind
the shivering shades of a nightmare.
Take time to change your mindset,
and heal your thoughts
with love,
wisdom,
and patience.
All along your journey,
my poems will be here

to comfort and support you.
All along your journey,
my words will open their arms,
hug your heart,
and tell you this simple truth,
"You are precious and worthy of love.
You are able to defeat the tigers
that live in your mind,
and *turn your heart into*
a peaceful oasis."

Taming the Tigers Within

This life is a harsh jungle
filled with multiple traps,
challenges,
and beasts.
But you are not meant
to sit on a couch
and watch the jungle from afar
as a spectator.
You are meant
to pass through this jungle,
combat the wild beasts
you encounter,
and tame any creature
that scares you.
You have the strength
to overcome all challenges,
escape any tricky trap,
head bravely to hope,

and win peace and joy.
You are here
to create beauty from the chaos
and generate love and goodness
from darkness and fear.
You are here
to embrace your vulnerabilities
and change them into strengths.
You are here
to bring to heel your inner tigers
through willpower
and wisdom.
You are here to become a hero
in a harsh jungle
filled with multiple traps,
challenges,
and beasts.
And with every new step you take
through the jungle,
my poems will be with you
as a sign of loving support –
I am here too,
and we are wonderfully brave.

Alexandra Vasiliu

Healing Comes in Peace

Push aside the veil of words
and step into the miracle of silence.
When two broken souls meet,
no words are needed.
Let's sit close to each other,
quietly carrying our stories
as we would carry secrets.

Don't be afraid.
Listen to the sounds of silence.
Healing comes in peace.
Stay with me,
I will stay with you
and hold your hand.
Our hearts will say
everything and anything
they need to say.
Sharing stories with no words
is a form of trust and love.
Be quiet now.
Let's trust each other.
You are anxious,
I am calm.
Our hearts will meet
in a beautiful place
where no words are needed.
Stay with me,
and I will stay with you.
There will come a moment
when we realize
we have been stronger than our traumas.
We have been fighting
to be confident and hopeful again.

Pull Worries Out by the Roots

Your heart is a garden,
and it's your choice
how you keep it.
You have two major options:
be a keen gardener or
an incorrigible loafer.
You can also consider the third option –
to take some care of your garden,
but never devote too much time.
In this case,
you can never be able
to remove anxiety
from your heart.
If you choose to be a dedicated gardener,
you will always take care of your heart.
You will seed the wonderful flowers
of self-awareness,
inner strength,

and courage.
You will water them
with love
and empathy,
and nurture them
with self-acceptance
and understanding.
In each corner of your garden,
you will cultivate the plants
of hope
and determination.
Wherever you see the weeds
of self-doubt,
self-sabotage,
or fear,
you will be quick to remove them.
You will pull them out by the roots,
and not allow them to grow
and become the dominant plants
of your garden.
You will be vigilant,
keeping your inner garden beautiful,
bright,
and peaceful.
And when you want

to spend some time with yourself,
you will go inward
and admire a gorgeous haven,
full of positive emotions
and vibrant colors –
the colors of inner strength.
You will be so thankful
for what you created.
But if you choose to be a loafer,
you will abandon your heart
and roam around aimlessly.
The toxic plants of low self-esteem
and the invasive weeds of anxiety
will gain a foothold
in your inner garden.
Thousands of negative thoughts
will suffocate your hopes,
and all kinds of fears will intoxicate
your dreams.
One day,
you will realize
your heart is a mess,
and you will be suffering immensely.
What can I do from now on?
you will ask yourself.

My friend,
run away from complacency
and self-sabotage.

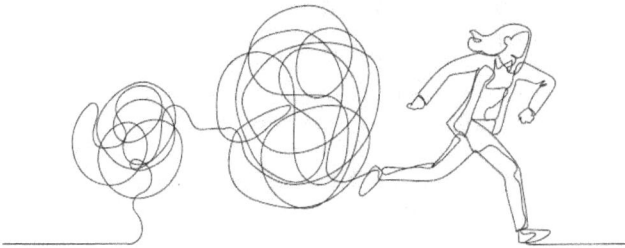

You are one decision away
from changing your life
for the better –
go inward
and work on your heart and mind.
There is always something to do.
Don't postpone this work.
Your garden is waiting for you.
You are the only one
who can keep your garden delightful.
You are the only one

who can understand
your emotional needs.
Heal your intrusive thoughts
with bravery and determination.
Every day,
seed positive feelings
and grateful thoughts,
and help them flourish.
Stop self-sabotaging
by exposing yourself
to what makes you scared.
You will realize
fears are not strong tigers –
they just roar in your mind.
But if you choose to confront them
and fight back
to tame them,
you will learn
they have no power.
You will realize
how incredibly strong and brave
you truly are.
On that day,
you will boldly translate your fears
into wisdom,

for no one keeps paper tigers forever.
You will embrace your inner child
with confidence and compassion.
You will realize
that you have been strong –
you have beaten your anxiety.
You will realize
that you turn anxiety into strength
and become your own hero.
From that day on,
you will spend many glorious moments
in your beautiful heart,
finding yourself in peace and joy.

Step Out of Your Inner Cave

If you isolate yourself,
the invisible tigers of anxiety
will eat you up.
Don't do that!

You are much more important
than the anxiety
you are experiencing right now.
Demolish the walls
that you built around yourself.
Escape your inner cave.
Open your heart and mind.
You are the best one
to offer a helping hand
to your inner child.
Give love and certainty
to your scared heart
and remind yourself,
Pure love always heals.
Demolish the walls
that you built around yourself,
and go toward the light.
No beast can stop you.
No snake can slither into your mind.
No tiger can run faster
than your brave heart.
Move forward with your life.
You are stronger
than the anxiety
you are experiencing right now.

Do simple things
that give great perspectives.
Visit a museum
or a beautiful ancient town,
and allow yourself to be in awe.
Go to a local botanical garden.
Have coffee with your best friend.
Take a painting class.
Sign up for a sports session.
There is no toxic creature
that can keep you trapped
in your inner cave.
Demolish the walls
that you built around yourself.
Allow my words to give you strength,
"You are incredibly precious and wise.
You are made
to humbly train any beast
to kneel before you.
There is freedom in your heart.
There is power in your mind.
Be bold.
This is your moment –
dare to quit your inner cave.
Dare to face anxiety.

Dare to wash away your toxic worries.
Dare to walk in the light.
No toxic thought can stop you
from thriving.
You are stronger than anxiety."

Handle This Harsh Season

If you feel invisible and insignificant
to those around you,
don't blame yourself.
It is not your fault.
It is nothing wrong with you.
It is about those around you.
They don't feel comfortable
with someone who thinks
and cares deeply.
Stay calm
and handle this harsh season of your life
with wisdom,
grace,
and understanding.
You are a deep feeler.
Remind yourself that
every winter lasts for a limited time.
If those around you

make you feel excluded,
don't abandon your beautiful self.
Stand up for yourself,
and show love to your precious self.
Invest time and energy in your worth.
One day,
you will no longer be invisible
and insignificant
to those around you,
for you have bravely dusted off
all your big dreams,
and audacious goals.
One day,
you will manifest your kind heart
and extraordinary potential.
But for now,
try to spend as much time as you can
growing
and preparing to shine.
You are essentially wonderful.

Alexandra Vasiliu

Give Emotional Food

When life gets chaotic
and you fall into a vortex of anxiety
and negative thoughts,
you ask yourself,
What is wrong with me?
Where could I find peace?

Have you ever acknowledged
that your heart has its own needs
like your body does?
Every day,
your heart gets hungry.
But your heart can never be full
if you nurture it with anxiety,
self-sabotage,
negative thoughts,
toxic relationships,
bad words,
and retail therapy.
You fool yourself.
Take a break
and reflect on your life.
Start a profound introspection.
What kind of life do you want?
What kind of relationship
do you look for?
What does your heart ask you every day?
How do you talk to yourself?
What ideals do you hold?
Be honest with yourself.
Pay attention to
what your heart tells you.

Cherish this catalytic moment.
Make peace with yourself,
detach from toxic people,
and start an emotional clearing process.
Give nourishing emotional food
to your heart –
love,
compassion,
and courage.
Feed your heart
with positive and consistent feelings –
it is the only way to find peace,
and build a beautiful life.
One day,
you will be thankful for your change.
One day,
you will notice
your heart is no longer starving,
for you have nurtured it
with healthy emotional food –
love,
self-awareness,
compassion,
wisdom,
strength,

peace,
acceptance,
and joy.
One day,
your life will no longer be chaotic,
for you have laid a strong foundation –
you chose to be present in your heart
and keep it bright,
pure,
and peaceful.
You are a brave and wonderful person.

Find the Bandwidth

Each time
you sabotage yourself,
you feel ashamed and guilty.
Stop self-flagellation.
Stop self-torture.
Stop doubting yourself.
Have you thought
that it is time
to search for a bandage
to put on your emotional
and mental wounds?
This bandage isn't
a *hocus-pocus* remedy,
its name is *inner work*.
Be persevering
and maintain an iron will.
Make peace with yourself,
fill your emotional hurts

with love and understanding.
There is no way
to change your toxic behavior patterns
without reaching forgiveness
and deep healing.
There is no magic bullet
that allows you
to leapfrog over these steps.
Do your inner work.
Be self-aware,
patient,
and consistent.
Step by step,
you will learn to become self-confident
and never sabotage yourself again –
the bandage of your *inner work*
will never fail again.
You are an incredibly strong soul.

Changed into Butterflies

Are you afraid of
what the future can bring you?
Are you afraid for your health?
Are you afraid of losing your loved ones?
Stop these worries now.
They sabotage your mental wellbeing.
Instead of
constantly pouring toxic worries
into your mind,
slow down and say humble prayers,
"God, please preserve my mental health.
God, please guard me
and my loved ones."
Your heart has angel stardust,
and you can change your inner storms
into butterflies
just by practicing the gentleness of prayer.
You will learn to become calm.

You Can Reach Inner Peace

Peace doesn't just embrace you
when all your problems have been solved.
Peace can open the door of your heart
in the middle
of an emotional storm.
My friend,
wherever you are now
with your life,
you can reach calmness.
Try to use these simple coping skills –
fill your days with love,
wisdom,
clarity,
empathy,
emotional safety,
and kindness.
Read a good healing book,
listen to some soothing music,

pray,
trust God more,
buy a bouquet of colorful flowers
for yourself,
help someone in need,
make your neighbor smile,
get together with your friends
and allow their trust to empower you,
pick fruits in an abundant orchard,
write a letter to someone you love,
do small, beautiful things
that can strengthen your mind and heart.
And peace will find you
and build a home in your heart.
Just let the light come into your life.

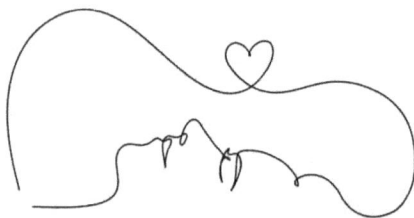

You Will Become an Alchemist

If you are wondering
how you can control and stop anxiety,
please embrace my words:
"Learn to forgive yourself and others.
Pray for that.
Stay busy spreading kindness.
Pray for that.
Nurture healthy friendships.
Pray for that.
Discover a hobby.
Do something you enjoy.
Focus on the bright side of life,
humbly anticipating the good things
that you can become."
You will not achieve
a successful result overnight.
It is a daily process of training yourself
into new and healthy habits.

It is a daily struggle to rebuild yourself.
It is a daily task
to transform your life,
heart,
and mind.
You will be the alchemist of your life –
you will use anxiety
like fuel
to create a new, strong, brave *you*.
Embrace this challenge
and pray for good results.
One day,
you will hug your heart
from a totally different place –
a haven
filled with wisdom and clarity.
One day,
you will realize
you become
what you've been feeding yourself with –
a river of love and peace.
You are already more than
whatever you leave behind.

Be Persistent

Sometimes,
change can bring failure.
Don't be discouraged.
We are not supposed to be successful
from the start.
Life is a chain of ups and downs.
Rise and try again.
You can try a hundred times
or a million times –
either way is okay.
You can fail a hundred times
or a million times –
rise and try again.
Don't be scared –
life is an obstacle course,
but *you are here to thrive on obstacles
and overcome challenges*.

Not Good Enough

When you afflict yourself
with the fear
that you are not good enough,
it is time to stop that kind of thought.
Please acknowledge it
as destructive thinking that sabotages you.
You are already good,
worthy of being loved and cherished.
You are already strong and brave
to recognize this thought
as toxic and sick.
So, please consider making
a mindset change.
When you think you are not good enough,
please ask yourself
if you seek validation from others.
If so,
please stop comparing yourself to others.

Stop comparing your life to others' lives.
Stop polishing your self-image
to comply with a social media standard.
It is a toxic need
that destroys self-esteem
and amplifies anxiety.
It is a poisonous need,
so please heal it.
Life is not about
who advertises their life better.
Happiness is not a competition.
You are already good and talented
at what you do.
Focus on your emotional growth,
and find healthy sources of joy.
Whenever you think
"I am not good enough,"
please don't believe that.
Say to yourself,
"I am beautiful and unique
in everything I am.
*I will keep growing
and blooming with kindness
at my own pace.*"

Alexandra Vasiliu

Add More Blessings

When life gets hard,
please remember this:
Anxiety is not your identity.
Your insecurities might last
for a short time,
but they don't have to overwhelm
or define you.
You are not your anxiety.
You came into this world
to grow beautifully,
to reach your full potential,
and add more blessings to your life,
your loved ones' lives,
and your community.
Don't overfeed your insecurities.
Don't introduce yourself
with these statements,
"I am anxious"

or "I have anxiety."
Instead, try this presentation,
"I am a flower about to bloom.
I have stars in my heart
that are about to shine."
Discover your strengths and qualities.
Focus on profound self-discovery
and improving your life.
Remain diligent.
And next time,
when you have troubles,
please return to your epiphany,
and repeat my words,
"I am a flower ready to bloom.
I have stars in my heart
that are ready to shine.
I am strong enough
to turn my fears into fortitude,
and add more blessings to my life,
my loved ones' lives,
and my community.
I am much more than anxiety and fears."

Don't Please Others!

When you please others,
you will open the door
to anxiety and emotional abuse.
You will write your personal story
with the hands of others.
Stop allowing others to dictate your life.
Stop seeking validation and approval
for everything you do.
You don't have to be compliant
in order to have good friends.
Take a break
and try to use the following strategies.
Find time for introspection
and reflection.
Discover yourself more.
Learn how to stand on your own feet.
Learn how and when to say *no*.
Keep your moral values,

and find your own spark.
Redefine your major goals.
Set boundaries,
and slow down the hurley-burley
of your everyday life.
Spend time
in the most rewarding
and beautiful way –
create good habits
for your mental health,
and discover your unique worth.
You will thank yourself every day,
and everyone will respect you.
Your heart is a beautiful poem.

What If It Is Not?

Sometimes,
you fear
that something terrible is imminent.
But what if it's not?
What if the negative possible outcomes
never come true?
Do some deep breathing for five minutes.
Instead of feeding your worries
and imagining the worst-case scenarios,
start a counterattack,
using your strength,
hope,
and courage.
Think logically.
Visualize a moment of pure happiness.
Get outdoors
and take a stroll in the glorious sunshine.
Listen to the birds chirping.

Are they ever worried?
Watch the ants
carrying breadcrumbs
on their backs.
Are they ever worried?
Look at the small kids playing in the park.
Are they ever worried?
Now,
return your attention inward,
and say to yourself,
"I am grateful to witness
all these wonders of life.
I am thankful to be alive
and start over my life.
I want to embrace my inner child,
with these words –
You need love and joy.
I will work on myself
to give you all these blessings
and create a peaceful life for you.
I am grateful for this revelation.
I am worthy of love and joy."

Take a Break

When social media creates anxiety,
why don't you take a digital detox?
People can praise themselves
on social media
without your applause or participation.
Be free of this nonsense.
Stop being riddled with social anxiety.
Take a social media break.
You will feel tranquil and happy
like a child born yesterday.
Your heart and mind will be eager
to rediscover
all the simple miracles of life.
You will have time
to heal your negative thoughts,
defeat self-sabotage,
and reconnect with yourself.
You will be able to find your own grace.

Encourage Your Inner Child

Random anxiety is an unhealthy way
in which your inner child tells you
that you need love,
comfort,
understanding,
acceptance,
confidence,
and a lot of healing hugs.
Leave aside all your fears,
and stay busy
mending your emotional health.
Make time for hugging
and encouraging your inner child –
Love is the shortest word for healing.

You Need This Lantern

If you can't find your peace,
worries will trigger more anxiety,
and anxiety will multiply worries.
It is an addiction you keep perpetuating.
How can you escape this toxic habit loop?
How can you step out of this vortex?

Start a journey of self-awareness.
Get to know your beautiful self more.
Try to go to the root
of your worries.
Understand yourself better.
Reflect more on your needs and desires.
Spend more time in nature
and enjoy its peace.
Every tree will tell you a story
about strength,
determination,
and patience.
Every flower will tell you a poem
about beauty,
peace,
and grace.
You need all these silent narratives
to reinforce your willpower
and learn to focus on peace
and positive thoughts.
And next time,
when worries arise,
don't let them manifest on autopilot.
Be forthright,
and command them,

Alexandra Vasiliu

Stop it.
Self-control is the lantern
that you need to roam freely
in the forest of your life.
Hold it,
and *you will become
the hero of your own story.*

Anxiety Is a Saboteur

Anxiety is a saboteur
who fearfully tells you
"Everything in life can be dangerous."
Lay back for a few moments.
Take deep breaths,
and allow life to flow
through your veins.
Look upon your heart.
Do you see
how wonderful you are?
Look beyond your anxiety.
Do you see your future
filled with beautiful surprises?
Take heart
and admit
that everything in life
is beautifully out of your control.
But you are called

to expand dreams
and embrace bravery.
*Dare to dream
and find your true spark.*

Everything Changes

Life shouldn't be a permanent distress,
or an unbreakable chain
of anxiety and panic attacks.
Life is a present
that you can open
with amazement,
hope,
and joy.
Sometimes,
you might deal with uncertainty,
new situations,
new people,
and possibly new places.
But all these can bring you opportunities
and wonderful surprises.
Don't be sluggish.
Don't let mental stagnation
get established.

Don't allow yourself to act as a victim.
Be determined
to improve your mental wellbeing.
Your resilience plays a pivotal role.
Please take my words to heart,
Life is linked to transformation
and growth,
and so are you.
You are meant
to embrace change and evolution.
You are meant
to experience transformation and growth.
Fear not.
Every caterpillar turns into a butterfly,
and so do you.
Make room for these personal transitions,
and guard my words,
Each growth leads to a more fulfilled life.
Allow growth and change
to happen in your life.
You are on the brink
of a magnificent transformation.
You will evolve into
a more exquisite version of yourself.

Embrace the Gift of This Day

Anxiety is just an emotion
in response to fears,
so ask yourself,
"What am I afraid of?
Why do I overthink?
How can I cut the addiction to worry?"

Work on self-awareness,
clarity,
and discernment.
Learn about your fears.
Are they realistic?
Dig deeper underneath.
What do you lack?
What does your heart want?
Discover your dreams and aspirations.
Who can I be if I am not anxious?
Every morning,
ask yourself,
How do I want to live this day,
fearful or calm?
Choose to be the person
you wish to become,
and choose not once,
but choose every day
and every minute of your life.
You will gradually tame
the anxiety monster.
You will slowly cease to overthink
and be swept along in negative emotions.
You will be free and strong,
and no longer believe what fear tells you.

Every morning,
you will look into a mirror,
and say to yourself,
"I want to live this day
with as much self-awareness,
discernment,
clarity,
temperance,
empathy,
and wisdom
as I can.
I want to embrace the gift of this day.
I want to become something other
than anxiety whispers in my ear.
I want to see the light
at the end of the tunnel
and make the most of my life.
I want to grow
and thrive.
I want to radiate confidence,
compassion,
love,
and grace.
I want to bloom."

Start Discerning

Has anybody told you
that not all your thoughts are important?
Many of them are superfluous
and come intermittently.
Learn how to discern them.
Let go of your unhealthy thoughts.
Have you found someone
who can stop the wind from blowing
and the clouds from sailing in the sky?
Neither can you.
Let go of your negative thoughts.
Stop paying attention
to all the discouraging thoughts
in your mind.
Stop paying attention
to all the toxic emotions
that arise in your heart.
Stop being the master of self-sabotage.

Stop acting like a leaf
blown in all directions
at once.
Become a master of wisdom
and empathy –
your mind and heart will thank you.
Start discerning your thoughts –
it is part of your journey
of self-discovery
and maturity.
Exercise your mind
to identify the thoughts
that guide you toward hope,
encouragement,
and self-confidence.
The easiest technique for that
is to start
a mental health journal.
You will meet your vulnerable self
in a secret, private place
where you can write down
your reflections,
your emotions,
your feelings,
your questions,

your concerns,
your wishes,
your worries,
and experiences.
It is the only place where
you can stop the wind from blowing
and the clouds from sailing in the sky,
where you can ask the moon
about her beauty
and the sun
about his courage.
It is the place
where you can calm your inner storms
and move safely forward.
Start a mental health journal today,
and you will discover
that all deterring thoughts have no power
over you
and they can't control you.
You are already remarkably brave.

The To-Do List to Overcome Anxiety

Keep your good sense.
Think logically.
Use your reason.
Find peace through prayer.
Make God your best friend.
Don't suffer in silence.
Talk to your family
and your best friend.
Take time to discover yourself
with the eyes of love,
not the eyes of fear.
Don't spend your days
stuck in your room.
Come up with ideas
about spending more time outdoors.
Be consistent
in maintaining good mental habits.
Cherish temperance.

Alexandra Vasiliu

Tune out of social media regularly.
Practice self-discipline.
Discover your hobbies.
Do an art craft weekly.
Listen to music every day.
Plant flowers.
Journal your emotions
and write down your thoughts daily.
Make a wish.
Be creative,
and nurture creative thinking.
Don't believe everything
that goes through your mind.
Don't overlook your need for kindness
and gentle words –
you want emotional protection.
Accept inner personal growth –
staying the same is debilitating.
Every day,
make baby steps toward change.
One step forward is greater
than no steps at all.
Be patient
and compassionate with yourself.
Heal your heart

at your own pace.
Appreciate your accomplishments
and the gift of the present moment.
Accept that
you are strong.
Encourage yourself daily.
You deserve something more than fear.
Dare to be brave with yourself.
Dare to be strong for yourself.
One day,
life will reward you.

Say *No* to Anxiety

By saying *no* to anxiety,
you will say *yes* to hope.
By saying *no* to negative thoughts,
you will say *yes* to healthy thinking.
By saying *no* to self-sabotage,
you will say *yes* to self-esteem.
By saying *no* to emotional distress,
you will say *yes* to sanity.
By practicing all these mental exercises,
you will build courage and resilience.
A strong and perseverant mindset is all
you need
to navigate through life's obstacles
and find peace.
Cultivate bravery by learning to say no.

Don't Waste Your Heart

Anxiety is a demon
that pushes you away
from who you truly are.
This demon likes to torture you
and make you feel
like you walk on eggshells.
Nothing is safe for you anymore.
This demon rules your mind and life.
This demon wants to alienate
and block you from
reaching your potential.

My friend,
don't waste your kind heart on fear.
Your heart is a precious flower –
please don't abandon it
into the darkness of fear.
Stand by your heart.
Discover your worth.
Understand your emotional needs.
Grow roots in wisdom
and compassion.
Accomplish good things
that boost your self-confidence.
Be brave,
and slam the door of your heart
in anxiety's face.
Give oxygen to your heart –
dare to pray and hope.
You will learn
to turn your insecurities into strength.
This is the way
to make the demon of anxiety shrink
and disappear.
You are a bold ray of light.

One Choice

When anxiety visits you,
ask yourself,
"Is it rational
to pay more attention to
these constant nightmarish worries
than to my strong ambitions?
Do I care more about anxiety
than my noble dreams and aspirations?
To which should I dedicate myself?"
Choose only one.
Don't be anxious about making a choice,
be self-aware and determined.
You will live with your decision.

It Is Okay

If you are worried and scared now,
I want you to know
that your feelings and emotions are valid.
It is okay how you feel.
It is okay how you feel
about how you feel.
Everyone is unique,
so I will not tell you,
"Try to get over it,"
instead, I will say,
"Take all the time you need
to understand what happened.
Take all the time you need
to embrace healing and peace.
Take all the time you need
to embrace your authentic *you*."
Your fearless heart will shine beautifully.

It Is a Sign

When you worry too much,
it is a sign
that you care too much.
It is a sign
that you have a kind,
loving,
and sensitive heart.
It is a sign
that you tend to give all of you.
My friend,
you are a beautiful soul.
Why don't you consume
all your energy,
feelings,
thoughts,
attention,
and time
in a good direction?

Alexandra Vasiliu

Nobody can say,
"This river is bad
because it flows in a different direction."
The river is not bad,
it flows where it flows.
But you are an intelligent human being.
Your heart is a gorgeous,
young,
and tumultuous river.
Don't waste your life
flowing toward a dead-end.
You can change the way
you think,
feel,
and give your love.
Start healing your precious self.
Fashion your life
with gratitude,
determination,
and hope,
so one day,
your heart can meet the ocean of joy.

Start Healing Your Thoughts

When anxiety starts to manifest,
you get a lot of weird symptoms
because you somatize
what your thoughts dictate to you,
Fear!
Fear!
Fear!
Have you ever thought
that you are not supposed to be enslaved
to anxiety and self-sabotage?
Have you ever thought
that you deserve something other
than insecurities and darkness?
Have you ever thought
that you are meant
for a life of bravery?
Get up, my friend,
and start healing your thoughts.

Alexandra Vasiliu

Look into a mirror today –
you are a beautiful and young soul.
You were born for a life of courage,
honor,
and meaning.
You were born to thrive,
change,
and grow with perseverance.
All these processes involve struggle,
but you are stronger
than you can imagine.
Move on
and act bravely.
You are a beautiful and daring soul.

Never Say This

When worries pop up in your mind,
don't greet them with,
"Hey, welcome back!
Long time no see."
Never say this.
You need inner peace
to build a better life.
You need clarity to discover yourself.
You need self-awareness to create
something beautiful and meaningful
with your torn life.
So, instead of being polite to anxiety,
stay firm
and tell your worries
only one thing,
Stay away from me.

The Important Thing

Have you ever noticed
the important thing about anxiety?
It never tells you kind things
about yourself,
your family,
your friends,
your life.
It always shows up to batter your mind
with mean statements.
"You are not good.
You haven't done anything with your life.
You don't deserve respect.
You are sick.
Nobody cares about you."
Your worries come only to destroy you.
Your worries never tell you
even one kind word.
Anxiety never whispers in your heart,

"You are a good person.
You have done many great things
with your life
so far.
Your heart is healthy,
for you haven't hurt others.
Many people love you
and care about you.
You deserve love and respect."
Anxiety never participates
in your personal growth.
So why do you give it credit daily?
Why do you bend your ear
to its damaging words?
Why do you believe its lies?
Turn your back on anxiety,
and break its toxic loop.
Surrender yourself to courage
and kindness –
*you will do amazing things
with your life.*

Train Yourself

Life is not about being happy all day.
Life is not about being entertained all day.
Life is hard.
Life will punch you in the face
and knock you to the ground
when you least expect.
No social media post
and no ideology agenda will help you
in those lonely moments.
You will have
to look straight into the eyes
of your trauma,
and go through hell
to find an exit ramp.
Life is unmerciful.
Don't ever think
it is going to be a funny movie.
Life is hard.

Life is not about being happy all day.
Life is not about being prosperous,
excited,
or entertained all day.
Develop common sense.
Stop fantasizing.
Stop overthinking irrational things.
Come down to earth
and heal your thoughts.
Train yourself mentally and emotionally
to overcome life's challenges.
Sooner or later,
you will realize
that you need a bridge
of inner strength,
courage,
and ethical values.
Walking on this kind of bridge,
you can overcome life's hurts.

Alexandra Vasiliu

Overcome Your Fears

Are you afraid of starting a new day?
Are you afraid of school exams?
Are you afraid of making choices?
Are you afraid of trusting people?
Are you afraid of trusting people again?
Are you afraid of letting friends
into your heart?
Are you afraid of betrayal?
Are you afraid of heartbreak?
Are you afraid to love?
Are you afraid to love again?
Are you afraid of showing your feelings
for someone dear to you?
Are you afraid of rejection?
Are you afraid of what others think
of you?
Are you afraid of people gossiping
or judging you?

Are you afraid for your health?
Are you afraid for the health
of your loved ones?
Are you afraid of socializing?
Are you afraid of starting a conversation?
Are you afraid of leaving a place?
Are you afraid of being afraid?
Are you afraid of having a life
of permanent fears?
If your answer is *yes*
to any of these questions,
you are not alone.
We all have fears,
although we master them differently.
Some of us practice self-control,
others pray more,
while others fight back,
overcome one fear at a time,
and defeat one negative thought
after another.
Any technique you choose,
I am here to remind you –
you are capable of
making good decisions.
Anxiety can't define you.

Alexandra Vasiliu

Don't Open That Door

Someone said that anxiety is a visitor
that comes and goes.
But have you noticed
that you never enjoy its company?
Its presence makes you feel sad,
hopeless,
lethargic,
lonely,
grumpy,
and uninspired?
So, why do you keep opening
your heart's door
to let this intruder in?
Stay busy doing something you enjoy
and you won't hear the doorbell ringing.
Anxiety, I am not home for you.

Do More Internal Work

You spend so much time
talking about anxiety,
worries,
insecurities,
mental challenges,
and therapy advice.
But you spend so little time
talking about what truly matters to you,
about what you really desire,
and about what you believe
can change your life
for the better.
You seem to ignore
all these needs deliberately.
You hide yourself
behind so many fears.
Peel the worries away
from your mind.

My friend,
your worth is beyond anxiety
and fleeting concerns.
Discover your deepest desires
and invest in
what truly matters to you.
Heal your thoughts
and feelings
by listing all the reasons
you should be thankful
that you are alive.
Have the courage
to be grateful –
it is not easy.
Dare to shine with gratitude
and calmness.
You are a wonderful soul
with so many dreams and gifts
ready to be shared
with the world.
Talk less about anxiety and self-sabotage,
and do more work inward.

Outgrow Fear and Overthinking

Have you ever thought
that overthinking is the older sister
of perfectionism?
You analyze the same thing
sixty times a minute.
You imagine adverse outcomes
sixty times a second.
Stop sabotaging yourself–
you exhaust yourself
and push your mind to the brink
of a catastrophic depression.
Stop fueling your ego
with perfectionism
and self-criticism.
Stop living
with a radical sense of entitlement
that everything in your life
should be easy and perfect.

Train yourself
to find simple solutions to any problem.
Train yourself
to become a simple and humble person.
Train yourself
to become a joy to others.
Train yourself
to grow a heart
full of kindness and understanding.
Simplify your life.
Pray to God to teach you.
Don't strive to build a 'perfect' life.
Instead, you should endeavor
to change yourself
and become a more carefree person.
Heal your perfectionistic thoughts
with this simple and humble affirmation,
I am wonderfully imperfect –
that is core
to outgrowing fear and overthinking.
Your courageous heart has the power
to conquer anything
that is self-destructive.

Fight the Good Fight

Why do you waste time
thinking of bad things
that might or might not happen?
Why don't you ever imagine good things
happening to you?
I know
that you are struggling
to get to know your worth.
I know
that all you need is
to feel safe and loved.
Please consider
putting into practice these strategies –
block any devaluing self-affirmation
and let go of self-doubt and self-pity.
Start holding on to positive thoughts
and embrace your strengths.
Accept your vulnerabilities

as a sign of authenticity.
You will become what you think,
so think good things about yourself
and bring them off.
If you think you are a good person,
do good things for yourself and others.
If you think you are a kind person,
spread kindness and love
in your heart
and to those around you.
Respect this commitment,
and you will nurture healthy self-esteem.
Don't expect passively
to become a better person.
Don't expect good things
to happen to you
without your contribution.
Fight the good fight,
and you will be able
to say *goodbye* to negative thoughts
and *hello* to genuine personal growth.
You are already capable
of a remarkable metamorphosis.

Start Praying

Have you ever thought
that struggling with anxiety
is a good reason
to start praying to God
and ask for support,
help,
and guidance?
You are not only your body.
You are a ray of light,
a caring heart,
and a profound mind,
wrapped in a human body.
Be authentic and sincere in your prayers,
and God will invigorate you
to overcome your trials.
*You are an extraordinary piece
of divine power.*

Stay Grounded

Have you ever realized
that anxiety never fixed your problems?
Anxiety uses a magnifying glass
that hyperbolizes your worries.
Sometimes,
anxiety makes you focus on things
that haven't occurred yet
and might never happen.
My friend,
it is time
to stop feeding your heart and mind
with toxic food –
endless worries and concerns.
Reorient your thoughts and heart
toward something real,
useful,
and appealing.
Devote yourself to beautiful ideals.

Do something meaningful
and noble
that can restore your inner peace.
Stay grounded.
Begin a spiritual journey.
Seek God.
Search for profound answers,
and find a solution to your actual trials.
You are not designed
to live a life of fears
and unsolved problems.
You are called
to nurture your heart and mind
with harmony,
and spread joy around you.
Remember,
your heart is a beautiful miracle,
filled with a myriad of feelings.

Write It Down

When you feel down,
and anxiety hurts you,
write down four healing affirmations.
I am brave.
I can let go of any stressor.
I want to love and be loved.
My safe home is my peace.
You may now visualize yourself
as a brave fighter
who comes up
with a promising solution
to your negative thoughts.
Remember one word
from these healing affirmations –
peace.
Build your dreams and life
around this powerful word.
Open your heart,

take a deep breath,
and look out of your window –
have you noticed
the flowers just bloomed?
Start your new life today.
Your safe home is your peace.
You can love and be loved.
You can let go of any stressor.
You are brave.

Alexandra Vasiliu

Don't Believe in Lies

You can't control everything in your life,
but you can control
what you do with your heart.

You can control
what thoughts
you keep in your mind
and what feelings
you store in your heart.
In order to have charge of that,
learn to say *no* to anxiety.
Include these techniques
in your daily routine –
don't believe all the scary whispers
that come through your mind.
Don't believe the predictions
that fear keeps telling you.
Don't believe in lies.
Don't believe in false alarms.
Anxiety doesn't have a crystal ball,
so please don't let anxiety rule you.
Don't let anxiety set the rules
and dictate your life.
Don't open the door of your heart
to irrational worries.
Learn to say simply *no*.
If you don't know
where to begin in this learning process,
remember a rule from your childhood –

Alexandra Vasiliu

don't talk with strangers.
So, don't talk with anxiety,
self-doubt,
and self-sabotage.
They are strangers.
They are not part of your beautiful soul.
Don't open the door of your heart
to them –
they will never bring you flowers.

Become Your Best Ally

When worries try to weigh you down,
recognize their duplicitous voices
and say to yourself
"I am not the sum of toxic thoughts
that sabotage me.
They can't define me.
I am not the sum of hostile inner screams
that sabotage me.
I am not a vortex of anxiety.
Anxiety can't define me."
Try to change the relationship
you have
with your thoughts.
Try to heal your harmful thoughts.
Get in the driving seat
and head toward *hope*.
You will become your best ally
if you believe in yourself.

You are the magical sum
of bright emotions,
deep feelings,
sincere prayers,
and thousands of dreams
and aspirations.
You are a wonderfully unique ray
of light –
inner beauty can always define you.

Use This Key

When was the last time
you felt grateful?
Take your time
and create a list of ten things
that you are thankful for.
Every week,
read this list again.
Each time you go over it,
you will feel emotionally safe
and capable
of defeating your inner demons.
Gratitude is a mysterious key
that opens the door
to peace
and courage.
Find this fabulous key in your heart.

Visualize Your Future Self

Healing from anxiety is absorbing,
frustrating,
and challenging,
but don't give up.
Imagine who you will become one day –
a strong person
with a free and healthy mindset.
That is beautiful and rewarding,
so *keep working on yourself.*

Start a Soul Care Journey

People talk about sleep hygiene
and healthy food benefits
as mechanisms to cope with anxiety.
Have you noticed
that nobody is brave enough
to affirm
how powerful prayer is?
It cleanses your soul
and fills your heart
with peace
and hope.
Can you find more significant benefits?
Pray more, my friend.
Day after day,
you will realize
that you don't have to believe everything
you think
and you don't have to follow

every emotion
that pops up in your heart.
You just need to pray
and be covered by softness.
Pray.
You will learn to discern
the good from the bad.
You will build a balanced life,
and a stronger self.
You will restore your confidence
and journey toward peace and joy.
Pray more, my friend –
this is the number one strategy
for your mental and emotional hygiene.
Start your soul care journey today,
and include prayers
in your daily schedule
to conquer anxiety.
Embrace each moment
with wonder and love.
You are made to live joyfully
like an innocent child.

Something Meaningful

If you constantly think of
what others think of you,
please let me be honest with you –
you don't have a great goal in life.
You spend time seeking approval
from busy people
living their own lives.
Why don't you spend your days
trying to achieve something meaningful?
You are a soulful person.
Reclaim your true potential
and put your heart into
something essential.
Be an intentional achiever,
and embrace your awesomeness.
You have so many things to achieve.

One Attitude

Have you ever thought
that much of your suffering comes
from the stories
you keep telling yourself?
Have you ever thought
that you yourself created your pain?
You are the author of your anxiety.
My friend,
stop this psychological self-flagellation.
Stop giving credit
to each of your unrealistic thoughts
and catastrophizing situations.
Try to become mindful of
your thought patterns,
and replace your negative thoughts
with uplifting ones.
Accept the uncertainty of things
with courage and resilience.

Remind yourself
you are made to leave a beautiful trace
on earth –
and that trace will be your answer
to all the harsh obstacles of life.
So spend your time weaving love,
empathy,
clarity,
and meaning
into one result –
you.
Inspire yourself
with beautiful things,
and craft the narrative
of your life
with passion,
intention,
and purpose.
You can become
the best author of your life.

You Are Already Courageous

It takes courage to beat anxiety,
and you are already courageous
to want to defeat this monster.
My friend,
take heart
and manifest
what is best in your soul.
Don't waste your life
overthinking
and staying frozen in anxiety.
Spread your light
without preventing others
from spreading their own light.
Keep changing yourself for the better.
The more you fight against anxiety,
the more courageous you become.

Give Your Heart

Instead of being engaged in fear
and negative thoughts,
let your heart absorb my words,
Do something meaningful for others.
Offer joy to those you love.
Give time and attention
to those special people in your life.
Make someone smile.
Volunteer for a noble cause.
Spend a few hours
using your skills for others.
Embrace a mindset
of compassion and giving.
This is the most realistic approach
to breaking down anxiety.
Embody generosity –
you were designed for that.

When You Outgrow Anxiety

If you want to live the best of your life,
do something meaningful
with your precious self
and unique life.
Don't spend every day
worrying excessively.
You distort your own reality.
Step away from this dramatic way
of thinking.
Set new, beautiful goals.
You need perspective in life.
Ask yourself,
"What do I want to become
when I outgrow anxiety?"
Embrace your response,
and focus on your dream.
You can achieve extraordinary things.

Your Thoughts Are Not Facts

What triggers your anxiety?
If your answer is
"Troublemaking reasoning,"
let me remind you of one thing.
Your thoughts are not facts.
Your thoughts are clouds
that come and drift away.
You turn unrealistic thoughts into fears,
eliminating any filter.
You change each cloud into a major flood
and move yourself to an irrational reality.
Start healing your thinking.
Untangle yourself from toxic thoughts.
Return to a realistic life
where setting intentional goals is worth
all your attention.
You can build
a more purposeful existence.

Your Heart Is Not a Train Station

Each emotion is a visitor
that comes with its own baggage.
Some emotions carry heavy baggage
and want to stay with you forever.
But would you feel comfortable
living with anger or anxiety
for the rest of your life?
Stay at your heart's door
and say,
"I am sorry, anger.
I am sorry, anxiety.
I don't have room for you."
When hope visits you,
hold the door for her.
Open your heart
and let her in.
My friend,
all you need is acknowledgment.

Be always self-aware,
and practice self-reflection.
Emotions are just visitors.
You don't have to reject them,
deny,
bury,
or shut them down.
Acknowledge each of your emotions,
but don't let them all in.
Your heart is not a train station
where any traveler is welcome.
Learn to set boundaries
and create a safe place
for your loving self.
You can unlock the path
that leads you to hope and tranquility.

Alexandra Vasiliu

How Do You Talk to Yourself?

Do you talk to yourself
in a discouraging way?
That is known as self-sabotage.
Stop being judgmental of yourself.
Stop self-criticism
for you only increase negativity
in your life.

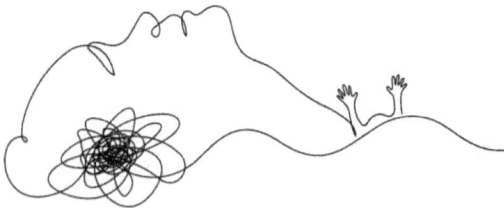

My friend,
it is time to change your behavior.
Replace the recurring habit
of poor self-talk
with encouraging and kind self-talk.
Be the first
who believes in yourself
and your potential.
Fill your days
with motivating activities,
and constantly remind yourself,
"I am a brave and joyful spirit.
My heart is brimming with dreams,
simply waiting to be shared
with the world."

Alexandra Vasiliu

Your Heart Will Turn into a Flower

Do things that add light to your soul,
and never leave morality out of your life.
Prune away anything convoluted
or obscure
that darkens your soul.
Turn your heart into a flower.
A flower of light and color.
You will realize
that this is why you are here,
this is why you were born.
To grow in inner beauty.
To do things that add light to your soul.
To leave valuable and bright traces
in this world.
To stand out in the purest,
most beautiful,
and righteous way.
Your heart will flourish with grace.

Your Heart Is Precious

When you stumble in the darkness,
I hope
you remember my words,
There is light within you.
Rise from the depths of darkness
and embrace the light within you.
Your heart is beautiful and precious.
Never let anyone destroy
your self-confidence,
especially if that person is you.

Don't Torture Yourself

Don't allow negative thoughts
to bring you down.
Don't allow anxiety
to invade your mind
and push you toward a spiritual drought.
Don't torture yourself.
Don't allow the angel of determination
to abandon you.
When you see these bad habits
harming
and persecuting you,
get up
and fight
with all your might
for your mental health.
Fight for your healing.
Fight for your inner peace.
Fight against negative thoughts.

Fight against self-sabotage.
Fight against self-doubt.
Fight against anxiety.
Fight against irrational fears.
Fight for what is good,
bright,
and pure
for your heart.
Deepen your inner strength,
and you will find peace
and freedom
in your healing journey.
You are stronger than anything
that tries to dim your inner light.

Keep Your Heart Clear

As you try to eat healthy foods,
do the best you can
to keep your heart clear from
emotional pollution –
toxic emotions,
negative thoughts,
overthinking,
self-sabotage,
and anxiety.
Never feed your heart
with these toxic things.
Give her the oxygen of harmony
and love.
Parent your heart with care,
wisdom,
and compassion.
You will be emotionally healthy.

Look Up

The stars shine at night
even when you don't look up at them.
The same applies to your dreams –
your aspirations are beautiful
even when you don't give them attention.
Why don't you start
working on them?
My friend,
don't postpone achieving
your aspirations.
Stop sabotaging your potential
and being dragged into negative self-talk.
Find the inner strength
to believe my honest words,
There is something great
waiting for you –
your aspirations.
Step beyond your dark comfort zone,

and pursue your dreams.
Let your inner desires
and ambitions shine
within you,
akin to the radiant stars
in the nocturnal sky.
Chasing your dreams will illumine you.

Be Gentle with Yourself

There are days
when you feel you are not strong enough
to go through
all life's suffering and anxiety.
Don't overthink that.
Don't blame yourself.
It is okay to feel tired
of being strong every day.
Take a deep breath
and hold on to my words,
Guard your soft heart
and absorb the grace of humility.
Tomorrow,
you will be ready to start over.
Tomorrow,
you will retake the helm of your life.
You are a brave and resilient soul.

Encapsulate One Word

If you could encapsulate your inner world
within one word,
don't let it be chaos,
despair,
darkness,
or anxiety.
Take your time
to heal yourself emotionally.
One day,
your heart could embrace again
only one word –
let it be joy,
peace,
or love.
You were created for a serene existence.

Your Sensitive Heart

If you are struggling with anxiety,
remember my words.
Get involved in
creating something beautiful.
Touch the world with your heart.
Help out someone in need.
Heal a broken heart
through love,
compassion,
and kindness.
Make someone smile.
Order ice cream
for all your neighbors' kids.
Learn a new language.
Take a class in painting or music.
Cook a meal for someone sick.
Do something beautiful.
Spend time outdoors.

Alexandra Vasiliu

Reconnect your inner child
with the purity of nature –
don't underestimate its healing power.
Hug a tree.
Smell the fresh grass
or a bunch of roses.
Listen to the silence.
Imprint that peace on your heart.
Gaze at a hardworking ant
and rethink your problems.
There is nothing unsolvable.
Just do your inner work.
Stop lingering in negative thoughts.
You were not born
to spend the rest of your life
in the dark forest
of anxiety.
Make an effort
to start every day
with positive,
proactive,
and inspiring thoughts.
Stay busy spreading kindness,
and transforming your heart
into a wonderful garden.

Every morning,
allow my words to wake you up
and motivate you
in your struggles
with overcoming anxiety,
My friend,
get involved in
creating something beautiful.
You were born
to touch the world with your heart.
In the grand tapestry of life,
there is nothing more important
than what you do
with your sensitive heart.
You are much more precious
than you think.

Remove This Mental Roadblock

If anxiety tortures you,
please consider making
a radical mindset change.
Stop seeking control of everything
that happens in your life.
Free yourself
from this toxic pattern.
That is not the answer to your fears.
Acknowledge
you can't control events in your life.
You can't control those around you.
Remove this mental roadblock,
and accept that
you are only a petal in this universe.
Feed your mind
with deep reflections.
Give your thoughts a positive purpose
to fight for.

"What shall I do with my life?
What kind of life do I want?
What ideals do I have?
What is the purpose I live for?
How can I grow in healthy friendships?
What can I do to increase
love and joy
in my relationship?"
Start doing something proactive
and meaningful
with yourself
every day.
Every positive, minor change,
consistently applied,
will shape your thinking
and elevate your life.
And next time
when anxious thoughts pop up
in your mind,
you will leave them alone.
You will be too busy
to start a conversation with them.
You will be too busy
choosing to improve your life.
You will be too busy

doing inspiring and healing things
for yourself.
On that day,
you will hug your heart
and say,
"I have no time
to entertain any of my fears.
I am busy healing my thoughts
and growing with confidence.
Anxiety is not my friend,
and this is why
I don't have to talk with her daily.
I need to prioritize quality time
with my true friends –
joy,
hope,
self-confidence,
self-esteem,
and courage.
I need to cultivate meaningful interactions
and move forward with my life.
One day,
*I will start spreading my light and grace
in this magnificent universe*."

Much More

If we become our thoughts,
don't become one
with your thoughts of anxiety.
You are much more than your anxiety.
You are much more than your sadness.
You are much more than your fears.
You are much more than your suffering.
You are much more than your screams.
You are much more than your loneliness.
You are much more than your darkness.
You are much more than your failures.
You are much more
than your resentments.
You are much more than your self-doubts.
You are much more than anything
you know about yourself
at this moment.
You are a ray of light and hope.

Alexandra Vasiliu

You are a poem of love.
You are a gift to the world.
Grow your precious self
with these healing affirmations.
One day,
your heart will shine again.

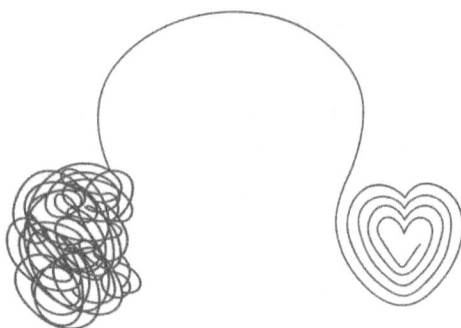

Different Voices

If you want to learn
how to unwind anxiety
and reverse all its damages,
learn to discern
the authentic voice of your conscience
from any other harmful voice.
Learn to identify
the pure and realistic messages
of your conscience
from all toxic illusions
that scare
and misguide you
in life.
Learn to filter all your thoughts.
Don't validate any harmful voice
that talks in your mind
and blocks you from
living your life to the fullest.

Alexandra Vasiliu

Cultivate those thoughts
that help you grow
and thrive.
In time,
you will learn to discern them all.

For now,
please accept
that this learning process is part
of your journey
of becoming a mature soul.
Be gentle with yourself along this journey.

Worrying Too Much

If you are worried about
worrying too much,
you are putting yourself
in an endless anxiety loop.
Please consider this truth –
don't stay in the trenches of fear.
It is time to accept
you can't have an answer
to every toxic question
that comes to your mind.
Try to live with the humbleness
of not knowing all the answers.
Try to live with the peace
of not raising constant questions
and unrealistic worries.
Be humble.

Get Up Stronger

There will be moments
in your life
when you feel unseen and rejected.
Don't despair.
Don't be sad.
Don't be anxious.
Be grateful for this opportunity
of reflecting on your life.
These lonely moments
when you question your life
are cathartic experiences
that help you cleanse your mind
and heart.
Use these unique moments
to prioritize your emotional wellbeing
and mental health.
Ask yourself,
How do I want to live from now on?

Stay away from toxic relationships.
Get to know your worth.
You are light.
Don't bury your heart in darkness.
Fill your cup with love and wisdom.
And when you feel unseen and rejected,
don't despair.
Don't be sad.
Don't be anxious.
Just tell yourself,
I matter.
This kind reminder will help you
reflect on your life
and put things in perspective.
You will be able to get up stronger
and work on your true worth –
every effort you put into your evolution
will make you feel seen,
accepted,
and loved.
You matter.

Alexandra Vasiliu

Change the Perspective

Picture anxiety as a shadow.
You can't run away from it.
You can't abandon it.
Accept that the shadow is still there,
and stop checking on it every minute.
Focus all your energy on
doing something beautiful
with yourself
and for yourself.
Move on
with your life.
With every new step,
that shadow is getting smaller
and smaller
behind you.
Change the perspective
of your emotional reasoning.
Start hoping.

Work on accomplishing your dreams.
You are wonderfully made
to grow with love
and thrive through positivity.
You are an extraordinary ray of light.

Be Grateful

Sometimes,
when you are happy or very excited,
you can get anxious.
You are afraid
that you could lose
the reason for your joy
or the person you love.
This type of anxiety is a special beast
that bites at the peace of your mind
and tears your heart out.
But there is a simple way
to tame this anxiety.
Replace the catastrophic thoughts
with thoughts and feelings
of gratitude.
It is not going to be
an easy, overnight change.
You need to be persistent

and practice gratitude
with self-awareness.
Each time you experience happiness,
be grateful.
Be thankful for every joyful moment,
and make efforts to preserve them.
Be grateful for having
a precious person in your life
that you love and honor.
And more important –
show your gratitude.
Don't just sit on your couch
and think,
"I should be grateful for this and that."
Show your gratitude diligently
whenever you can,
and this moment is one of these times.
Do small things
that can reveal your big, kind heart.
Remember this coping strategy –
when you practice gratitude,
you expel anxiety from your heart.

The Prescription for Anxiety

When you garden your heart,
you reduce anxiety
and negative overthinking.
Don't postpone this rewarding work.
Go inward
and water the soil of your heart
with meekness
and compassion.
Your heart will become soft,
strong,
and kind.
Plant gorgeous flowers.
You already know their names –
some are the flowers of hope,
love,
and compassion,
while others are the flowers of bravery,
wisdom,

and inner strength.
Each sweet flower is a perfect addition
to your garden.
Help them all thrive
and bloom all year long.
Help them grow
and spread their magical fragrance.
One day,
you will realize
that each beautiful flower
you planted
has been a remedy for reducing anxiety.
Go inward,
my friend,
and transform your feelings and thoughts
into bright flowers.
Bring peace into your life.
Plant the flowers of hope
and thankfulness.
Stay busy watering your soul
with healing and beautiful activities.
Keep gardening your heart,
and never mind about its aesthetic appeal.
Work on your emotional health
and positive thinking.

Cultivate a resilient mindset
focused on optimism,
growth,
healing,
and gratitude.
This is essential for you and your life.
My friend,
start your transformation today.
One day,
your heart will hold the nectar
of all your efforts.
And that will be such bliss.

You Have Been a Brave Fighter

You have been a brave fighter
for so long.
Now,
you can take the Band-Aid off
your wounds
and look straight into their depths.
You will see your past.
You will face your demons –
self-doubt,
self-sabotage,
anxiety,
and other toxic emotions.
But don't be afraid –
their low voices can no longer hurt you.
They are just shy inner naysayers,
ghostly voices
trying to destroy your self-esteem.
Please don't listen to them.

You have been a brave fighter
for so long.
Now,
you can look straight at these demons,
and yell at them,
"You couldn't put me down.
I crossed a terrifying minefield
filled with self-doubt,
self-sabotage,
anxiety,
and other toxic emotions.
I fought with you all,
and won!
I am free.
Now,
I can look back
and be proud of my achievements.
I won all your brutal battles.
I won.
I am free like an eagle."

You Will Understand

There will come a time
when you realize
that every good thing is a gift,
and every harsh thing is a lesson.
On that day,
you will see anxiety
through these lenses.
You will stop taking anything good
for granted.
You will stop letting anything tough
destroy you.
You will seed flowers
in the place where toxic thoughts arise.
You will raise butterflies
in the place where you fought tigers.
That will be your gift
to yourself.
On that day,

you will be grateful
you are alive.
You will say to yourself,
"I was able to tame my inner tigers.
I was able to control my anger.
I was able to overcome anxiety.
My life's obstacles were only lessons.
I am a gift to the world."

Healing Matters

My friend,
keep in mind
that healing a toxic mindset can take
a long time,
yet the rewards last forever.
If you want to heal
your destructive habits,
show compassion to your inner child.
If you want to heal
your intrusive thoughts,
start healing the words
that you say to yourself.
You are the first
who cares about your troubles,
so every step of your journey,
arm yourself with this truth,
My healing matters.

Alexandra Vasiliu

Expand Your Emotional Vocabulary

For an anxious mind,
there is one dominant word –
worry.
But to overcome fears,
you need to expand
your emotional vocabulary.

Please include these words
in your daily self-talk –
faith,
strength,
prayer,
love,
bravery,
gratitude,
encouragement,
perseverance,
patience,
trust,
hope,
dreams,
peace,
clarity,
generosity,
strength,
forgiveness,
healing,
acceptance,
friendship,
trust,
hugs,
empathy,

and joy.
Also, add the following adjectives
to your secret self-talks:
smart,
bright,
positive,
strong,
confident,
brave,
kind,
caring,
wise,
humble,
hopeful,
and empathetic.
Then, my friend,
please make sentences
with all these new words.
Combine them as you wish,
and compose uplifting phrases about you.
Please remember
that the way you talk to yourself
defines the way
you see life and its challenges.
Try to master these new words.

Include them emphatically
in your daily self-talk.
And each time
the word *worry* comes to your tongue,
fight back against this invisible beast,
and knock it down
with multiple empowering words.
You will be surprised
how quickly you will learn
the language of courage.
You will be able
to tame your inner tigers
through powerful and positive words.
You will become fluent
in a new language –
the language of the victorious.

My Wish for You

If fear sucks the joy from your life,
you may feel dull and apathetic.
You become emotionally distant
from your life.
You feel like a stranger
in a foreign country.
Allow me to ask you a brief question.
Do you want to spend
the rest of your life
in an emotional exile?
Start your healing journey today,
and return home
to your caring heart.
Show love,
compassion,
and understanding to yourself.
Be patient with yourself every day,
and today is one of those days.

Do little beautiful things
that can boost your self-esteem.
Make space for your dreams
in your daily life.

I hope
one day,
you will feel comfortable
in your heart again.

Alexandra Vasiliu

From that day on,
you will no longer feel anxious
and scared.
From that day on,
nothing will steal the joy of living
from you,
for you will be whole,
hopeful,
and calm again.
*From that day on,
you will be home.*

Dear Reader,

Thank you for reading my book. I am very grateful that from millions of books, you chose mine to accompany you on your journey of healing, change, and growth. I hope my poems showed you your inner beauty and motivated you to overcome fears and unlock your full potential. That is the greatest gift I can humbly offer to you.

If you enjoyed these poems, please recommend my book to your friends and write a brief review on Amazon. It helps me and other readers more than you can imagine. It also allows me to continue writing books. Thank you very much.

With love,
Alexandra

Alexandra Vasiliu

About the Author

Alexandra Vasiliu is the author of the bestselling poetry books *Dare to Let Go,* and *Healing Is a Gift*. Her poetry touched thousands of hearts around the world.

Alexandra double majored in Literature and French for her undergraduate degree before pursuing her Ph.D. in Medieval Literature. When she doesn't write, she enjoys gardening, playing chess, and spending quality time with her family.

You can learn more about her work by visiting her website: alexandravasiliu.net or her social media accounts:

Instagram @alexandravasiliupoetry
TikTok @alexandravasiliupoetry
Facebook @AlexandraVasiliuWriter
Pinterest @AlVasiliuWriter

www.ingramcontent.com/pod-product-compliance
Lightning Source LLC
LaVergne TN
LVHW021456080426
835509LV00018B/2310